VALUES
Things Worth Standing Up For

AMBASSADOR

Values - Things Worth Standing Up For
© Copyright 1993 Derick Bingham

Cover photo: Noel Davidson

Printed and Published by
AMBASSADOR PRODUCTIONS LTD.,
Providence House,
16 Hillview Avenue,
Belfast, BT5 6JR
U.K.

ISBN   0   907927   94 7

INTRODUCTION

To say that values are falling apart in our generation is an understatement. Everything seems to be relative in our day, nothing seems to be absolute. To find someone with a value system and to see them stick to it is rare in our generation. In education, in science, in politics, in the home, in the judiciary, one could be forgiven for believing that rules seem to be based on the question, "What can it do for me?"

Selfishness seems to rule under the maxim; "Look after Number One". Our generation is the generation of the zapper; the person who moves from T.V. channel to T.V. channel after the three minute boredom threshold has been exhausted. This generation, said Michael Ignatiff, has "The attention span of a flea". Self-centredness and shallowness is widespread and what T.S. Elliott said about his generation is even more relative to ours; he spoke of, "The hollow men".

Recently when I was trying to hold up a Biblical value system on a B.B.C. programme which included on its panel a Marxist, a Social Worker, and a South African University Lecturer, the Moderator of the programme accused me of "Living on the Planet Zob". Some of my fellow-panellists held out strongly that there can be no such thing as a shared value system for human beings.

In this study I want to maintain that there is a value system which is worth following and in which we can all share. I want to draw your attention to the character of Daniel living out his life in ancient Babylon according to a value system from which we can draw deep inspiration for our everyday living. I gratefully acknowledge the help of my friend, Professor David Gooding, who first gave me a key to the understanding of the value system that Daniel followed. It is, in fact, God's value system and it is unbeatable for true success, wholesome living and leads to the blessing of any individual who follows it.

Derick Bingham

"When a generation stops worshipping God it does not mean that they worship nothing it is that they end up worshipping anything."

CHAPTER ONE

VALUES
in appetite

Our study in values begins in the fabulous city of ancient Babylon. Here is a city occupying an area of two hundred square miles and is built on both sides of the Euphrates. It is protected by a double defensive wall reinforced with towers. To the outside of this wall, about twenty yards distant, is an additional defence wall of burnt brick set in bitumen. Access to the city is gained by eight gates, the most impressive of which is the Isthar gate. To reach it you have to pass down part of the great stone paved processional street which is about a thousand yards in length. It is decorated on either side with figures of lions in enamelled brick. Assyrian art is at its height at this period and the draftsmanship and execution of these animals indicates an advanced degree of artistic skill. There are some fifty temples within the city of Babylon.

In the midst of all this complex is situated one of the seven wonders of the world, the celebrated Hanging Gardens of Babylon. They consist of terraces supported on huge masonry arches, on which carefully tended gardens have been laid out at different levels. The interesting feature of these raised gardens is the fact that they are visible above the tops of the buildings, and provide a welcome contrast of greenery against an otherwise unrelieved background of white roofs or an expansive sky. A number of mechanical hoists provide the means by which water is raised to these elevated terraces.

In an enclosed area south west of the Isthar gate is the huge Ziggurat of Babylon which was closely linked with the Temple of Marduk in the time of Nebuchadnezzar. The Marduk shrine was by far the most ornate, being richly decorated with gold, alabaster, cedar wood panelling, and semi-precious stones. In all, Babylon at its height was the most splendid city of the world.

In the middle of all this is a young ex-patriot Jew who rises, with three of his friends, to a position of great prominence. He is a man of prayer who is not ashamed to believe what the Scriptures teach regarding the coming Age of Peace which will be brought by the Messiah. Even though Jerusalem was wrecked and he is an exile, he goes right on believing the Scriptures. The Temple might be demolished in Jerusalem, Nebuchadnezzar might hold him and his three friends captive in Babylon, but God through His prophet Isaiah has promised that He will bring Israel back from her seventy year exile in Babylon. Daniel believes God, even though there is precious little sign of His promise being fulfilled as he lives out his life.

We too can be like Daniel. Our Saviour and Messiah has promised to return to this earth of ours. Do we go on believing His promise even though our contemporaries mock us, saying "Where is the sign of His coming?". The promises of God are the foundation of God's value system. Though the earth itself should change, the mountains tumble and swirling floods rage, God, the Lord of Hosts always keeps His promises. Hitch your life to them and you won't be sorry.

Daniel and his three friends soar to the top in their exams in the University of Babylon. They do not just study the Bible, they are experts in the Chaldean language and literature and one day, right in the context of their education, they take their first stand for God's value system. They refuse to eat the food placed before them.

It all had to do with Jewish food laws. There were three areas where food was unclean to the Jew according to the Mosaic Law. There were clean and unclean animals. To eat unclean animals was to eat unclean food. Had it to do with hygiene? No, for Christ cancelled the Old Testament food laws for the christian and Paul stated that everything is to be received if it be received with thanksgiving. That certainly did not mean that pigs had become more hygienic in New Testament than in Old Testament days!

The whole purpose of this law was that it was symbolic. God was Holy and He expected His people to be holy. The physical rule of not eating certain foods was to teach His people deeper lessons. God was saying that there are some ways of satisfying our appetites that are unclean. Just look around you in our generation and see what has happened in the area of sexual appetite. A sexual appetite is perfectly healthy in itself and when expressed within the bounds God has put for it in His Word, it is obviously one of His greatest gifts to us. Yet when that appetite is fed in an unclean way, look at what happens. What are the subjects dealt with by most films and novels in our generation? They deal with rapists, adulterers, sadists, homosexuals, and every kind of sexual perversion on the face of the earth. You couldn't have a more unclean feeding of your sexual appetite than that which most video shops present.

Look at the area of the appetite of thirst. Millions are spent by the drinks industry to advertise alcohol with its subsequent social and domestic disasters. What is even dished up to our generation in certain areas of ballet and other aesthetic arts is anything but healthy for us.

It was also commanded of the Jewish people that they refuse all food offered to idols. Underlying this commandment was the question of loyalty to God. So it was that Daniel took very seriously the question of how he fed his appetites and where his loyalty lay. There was no mistaking it, though, that when Daniel and his friends said, "No" to the king's food, they were asking for their very lives to be taken.

What is the practical application of what Daniel and his friends did for our day and generation? The application is that Christians too must how that they are different by taking a stand for the wholesome feeding of their appetites. It does not mean that they are not to use their minds, though, does it? It was in the context of his education that Daniel took his stand for the wholesome feeding of his appetite. So Christians in our generation are not to be anti-intellectual and they must how that the mind matters in God's value system. Why? Because:

❖ We were created to think. (Psalm 32: 9; Jeremiah 8: 7).

❖ We will be judged by our knowledge and our response to God's revelation. (Jeremiah 25: 3, 4; John 12: 48).

❖ We need our minds in worship. (1 Corinthians 14: 13-19).

❖ We need our minds to exercise faith. (Matthew 6: 26).

❖ The mind is vital in the quest for holiness. (Romans 12: 2).

❖ The mind is vital in the preaching of the Gospel. (1 Timothy 4: 13-16).

❖ The mind matters in pastoral care as a shepherd seeks to feed the flock of God. (Proverbs 2: 1-6).

We are facing idolatry today as great as Daniel and his friends faced in the days when the Babylonians worshipped their god, Marduk. We must rise up and oppose it with our intellects and in the name of morality with God's help. Never forget that the young men who took their stand for God in Babylon were no intellectual slouches. Let's follow their lead and example.

CHAPTER TWO

VALUES
in science

We desperately need, in our generation, to bring our minds to bear upon one of the greatest challenges to our faith; it is the challenge that our contemporaries bring which says that science and the Bible are incompatible. We want to maintain that true science and the Bible are not incompatible. The proof of that can be found in the book of Daniel. In the second chapter Nebuchadnezzar calls all the scientists of the day around him. They may not have had the sophistication of present day scientists but they have at least studied evidence and drawn up theory from the evidence like any modern day scientist. Nebuchadnezzar has had a dream and he demands, on pain of death, that his scientists tell him his dream and its interpretation. In other words, he wanted them to tell him what he had dreamt about without revealing to them any of the details!

They wisely answered, 'There is not a man on earth who can tell the King's matter; therefore no king, lord or ruler has ever asked such a thing of any magician, astrologer or Chaldean and there is no other who can tell it to the King except the gods, whose dwelling is not with flesh.'

They were honest, weren't they? True science only deals with evidence. It's a bit like someone saying, 'Is there anyone for tennis?' and then someone asks, 'Why do human beings play tennis?' You can play a game of tennis according to the rules of tennis but the rules of tennis are not framed to answer the question as to why human beings play it in the first place. Science will tell you why the sky is blue and the grass is green, but it can't tell you why the sky or the grass or even you are here on earth in the first place. Science simply can't answer that moral question. The Bible will, though, for God has intervened in history and revealed the reason why we exist. That revelation is found in the Bible and with all our hearts we believe it to be a divine revelation.

So it was that Daniel is brought before Nebuchadnezzar and in no uncertain terms told him, 'There is a God in heaven who reveals secrets' and God intervened and told Daniel the 'pre-history' of Nebuchadnezzar by revealing what he had dreamed and the dream's interpretation. That's what God can do and the Bible gives us 'pre-history' and the ultimate meaning of life.

Don't you think there is a lot of so-called true science about today and it is not true science? It is, in fact, merely deductionism. Take, for example, Desmond Morris' book 'The Naked Ape', or Richard Dawkins' book 'The Selfish Gene.' Morris's thesis is that man can be regarded as nothing more than one of the apes and Dawkins claims man is a gene machine blindly programmed to preserve its selfish genes.

Now someone may say, 'If that is science I don't want it, it's nasty.' But, it all depends from what standpoint you look at it. It has been pointed out that if you put the human body alongside other pelts, it is only identifiable by its skin or if you look at the human body from the point of view of the gene, you will see that the human body really is out to preserve itself. That's true. Why shouldn't it?

Yet, this is the fallacy of reductionism. The example has been given of a microscope on an ink blob. You could say, 'That's nothing but an ink blob.' If you look at it in a wider context, it is part of a letter of the alphabet, the letter 'e'. If you look at it in an even wider context, that letter 'e; is part of the word 'independence' and that in its wider context is in the middle of an inflammatory article about politics! If one level systematically ignores the other, we will never find the truth.

We must stand up in our day and nail the fallacy that if you describe man as nothing but a mass of molecules or nothing but a population of nerve cells or nothing but a carrier of selfish genes, then you have invalidated other levels of the significance of man! That kind of reductionism is a disgrace to true science.

Science cannot provide an answer to the quest for the meaning of life. Stephen Hawking, the seriously disabled and yet incredibly brilliant and lucid Professor of mathematics at Cambridge University who now holds Sir Issac Newton's chair, said that he sees no need for a personal God but that the universe runs according to the law of physics. He spoke of this on a recent television documentary.

The same documentary showed Professor Hawking's wife claiming that it was her Christian faith which kept her going and helped her to dress, feed and get her husband ready for work! That little cameo was a metaphor of what we are trying to say in this study!

One thing is for sure: Daniel was not anti-science but he is showing the clear distinction between science and revelation. Put in modern parlance it's like a little boy who finds a pocket calculator in a field. He's never seen one before and he starts speculating. 'It's fallen from Mars,' he thinks. 'It's a power-gun,' he muses pointing at this school! On and on he speculates until the man who has invented calculators happens to come strolling by. 'Do you know what it is, sir?' asks the lad. 'Indeed I do,' he replies and reveals it all to the child. So it is that there is a very real difference between science and revelation. No one shows us that more clearly than Daniel.

So, in our study of Daniel chapters one and two, we have seen the importance of the values God would maintain for our aesthetic, intellectual, psychological, physiological and spiritual appetite.

We have seen God's view of science and the true value of His divine revelation. Let's ask Him, by His grace to help us to maintain them. God will hold us accountable for the truth about Himself that we have been exposed to in life. Let's be careful with that truth. Let's stand up for those values.

'Dare to be a Daniel?
Dare to stand alone?
Dare to have a purpose firm?
Dare to make it known?'

CHAPTER THREE

VALUES
in worship

'They shut the road through the woods,
Seventy years ago,
Weather and rain have undone it again,
And now you would never know
There once was a road through the woods.'

Kipling's poem describes perfectly what has happened to a very important question which has been overgrown by ten thousand other issues and which we should all be asking ourselves. The question is, 'Who owns me?' Let's investigate this question in the life story of Daniel. It all has to do with what we worship and the value we put upon worship.

In Daniel chapter three we read of King Nebuchadnezzar who puts up a ninety foot high, nine foot thick statue on the plain of Dura, and calls the 'higher-ups' in his empire to its dedication and commands them and all the people under his rule to bow down and worship it.

It is not very long before certain Chaldeans come forward to the King and declare, 'There are certain Jews who you set over the affairs of the province of Babylon: Shadrach, Meshach and Abed-nego; these men, O King, have not paid due regard to you. They do not serve your gods or worship the gold image which you have set up.' Why did Daniel and his three friends refuse to bow down to Nebuchadnezzar's gold image?

Because although they were prepared to live peaceably and quietly under Nebuchadnezzar's rule, obeying and administrating his laws, they believed they must worship God alone. Nebuchadnezzar is claiming for the state the absolute loyalty which they believed is due only to God. Worship in the ultimate sense means bowing down to ultimate authority. They believed God is that authority and that their loyalty was to him. They believed that God owned them. Do you? Is this a value which you stand up for?

You will remember that when Christ came to Israel He described the situation as being like the figure of a vineyard that God had let out to His husbandmen. They wanted it for themselves and even killed the son of the owner to get it. Notice what Jesus taught them; even if they did kill the owner's son, the owner was not giving up his claim to be the owner of the vineyard. Christ was saying that God is the ultimate owner of this earth and He has refurbishment plans. Notice that when Judas, Christ's disciple, thought he would strike out for himself, betray Christ and with the money he got for his treachery, he would buy and own some land, it led him to indescribable disaster. He forgot who owned the world and with blatant disloyalty to him, he bought a field. No wonder, the Bible tells us, it was turned into a cemetery after his suicide. All attempts to claim ultimate ownership of anything on earth without due reverence for the One who ultimately owns it will end in death, in fact, eternal death.

So it was that when Daniel and his friends wouldn't bow down to Nebuchadnezzar's image, it was not narrow-mindedness that made them do it. It was not sectarian ism or racial bigotry, they were striking a blow for true freedom because to be asked to bow down to a government or anything else, other than Almighty God, and worship it and give it ultimate and absolute support, spells a slavery and an indignity that is fearful to contemplate.

All around us in our generation, atheistic and materialistic theories are being taught. If people do not worship God then they must worship something. Standing in Moscow's Red Square many years ago my guide was telling me that there was no God. He only believed in his wife and children and family circle. 'Look, though, what you have put in God's place,' I said as we gazed at the body that they claimed to be the embalmed body of Lenin in the cool mausoleum. Soldiers guarded it. Many millions queued to see it. The Communist structure that my guide had so firmly believed in with all of its atheism has crumbled and Lenin and his co-hort's theories have been discredited, but, what a fearful harvest their poisonous seeds have brought! They engaged the people's loyalty to something which could never take the place of God.

We must never let anyone or anything force us to be disloyal to the One who owns us. We must stand up against it. It was Hitler and his Nazis who tried to take over the loyalty of the churches in Germany. The sad thing was that precious few objected. Listen to Pastor Niemoller: 'In Germany they came first for the Communists and I didn't speak up because I wasn't a Communist. Then they came for the Jews and I didn't speak up because I wasn't a Jew. Then they came for the Trade Unionists and I didn't speak up because I wasn't a Trade Unionist. Then they came for the Catholics and I didn't speak up because I was a Protestant. Then they came for me and by that time no one was left to speak up!'

Christian: if you would be strong when a big thing comes to challenge your loyalty, then be strong in the smaller things and cultivate the habit of regular decisions in the nitty-gritty of life to be loyal to your Saviour.

Was it costly for Shadrach, Meshach and Abednego to be loyal to their Lord? It certainly was. They were cast into a burning fiery furnace made hotter than normal to wipe them out. Did they think God would deliver them? 'Our God whom we serve is able to deliver us from the burning fiery furnace,' they said, 'And He will deliver us from your hand, O King, but if not, let it be known to you, O King that we do not serve your gods nor will we worship the gold image which you have set up.'

Notice a fine but very significant detail in this story. The Scripture says that, 'they fell down bound into the midst of the burning fiery furnace'. 'Look,' King Nebuchadnezzar says, 'I see four men walking loose, walking in the midst of the fire and they are not hurt, and the form of the fourth is like the Son of God.' Mark that word 'loose'. The bonds that bound them were loosened by God. It shows very clearly that the trial they went through freed them from the things that would have shackled them by holding a place in their affection and loyalty that only God Himself should hold. As Jim Elliot, the young missionary martyred by the Auca Indians in the 1950's in South America said, 'He is no fool who gives what he cannot keep to gain what he cannot lose.'

Daniel and his friends have taught us an invaluable lesson about what true worship is all about. They certainly became a mirror that reflected the glory of God. They stood up for the true value of worship and may we in our generation stand up for it too.

CHAPTER FOUR

VALUES
in culture

Culture is a very real thing. if you had been born, for example, in the England of Georgian times, you would not have moved very far from the village or town where you had been brought up. A trip abroad would have been a momentous event. In those days communities were closer and information spread very slowly. This affected the culture as it was expressed in art, fashion, architecture, education and social manners.

Nowadays the world has become a neighbourhood and information spreads via satellite and computer link-ups at unprecedented speeds. In the global money market more money changes hands in three minutes than the gross national product of the entire nations! In past times people had time, for example, to contemplate great art. Nowadays they have an attention span of about three minutes as television advertising clearly demonstrates. Everything has speeded up. All of this, of course, affects our culture in its state of manners, tastes and intellectual development.

The Book of Daniel has some very relevant things to say about the whole question of culture. A little concentration will show the teaching to be highly contemporary. We are told in Daniel chapter four that King Nebuchadnezzar has another dream while at rest in his house, while flourishing in his palace.

It is a dream of a great tree flourishing whose 'height reached to the ends of all the earth. Its leaves were lovely, its fruit abundant. And in it was food for all. The beasts of the field found shade under it, the birds of the heavens dwelt in its branches and all flesh was fed from it.' Then in his dream the tree is cut down with an angel saying, 'Leave the stump and roots in the earth ... in the tender grass of the field. Let it be wet with the dew of heaven and let him graze with the beasts on the grass of the earth. Let his heart be changed from that of a man, let him be given the heart of an animal and let seven times pass over him.'

What could it all mean? Daniel is called to interpret and the truth of the dream fills him with dread. God shows him that Nebuchadnezzar is represented in the tree and its stump. Daniel tells Nebuchadnezzar that he is going to 'be with the beasts of the field and they shall make you eat grass like oxen ... they shall wet you with the dew of heaven and seven times shall pass over you till you know the Most High rules in the Kingdom of men.'

It was strong stuff indeed. A year later Nebuchadnezzar is walking about the royal palace of Babylon. It is a very beautiful place. He is feeling very contented with himself saying, 'Is not this great Babylon that I have built for a royal dwelling by my mighty power and for the honour of my majesty?' While he is still the speaking judgment of God falls on him.

His sanity leaves him and he is driven away from human habitation. He eats grass like oxen, he couldn't care less about his clothes and his hair grows like eagles feathers and his nails like bird's claws.

You might think the story of Nebuchadnezzar weird but a moment's reflection will show that it is anything but weird. It is, in fact, extremely contemporary. The dream that Nebuchadnezzar had just had shows, by the interpretation given to Daniel, that God had by no means judged Nebuchadnezzar for building a beautiful city. Certainly not. God clearly showed that he though the city was lovely, that people obviously enjoyed it and that it gave them employment. God is not against beauty. Just look around you at the world He has created and you will see that He is into beauty in a big way. Even Solomon in all his glory was not dressed like a little flower of any field that God has created. Any of the fashion houses of the world cannot possibly compete with the beauty of God's couture. God is not a utilitarian, is He? Utilitarianism would teach that a thing is only good to human beings as it is useful to them. If that were so than a present of carrots, potatoes and parsnips would be a better present for your friend in hospital, than flowers! Thank God it is not so. Beautiful things lift the mind just because they are beautiful. Nebuchadnezzar was not judged just because he had built a beautiful city. He was judged because he had not shown mercy to the poor as he built it and because in the midst of all the culture he had created, he had forgotten God.

What is the significance of the fact that Nebuchadnezzar began to live like an animal? The answer is that when people forget God, a whole new thing invades their culture. They start living like animals, that is, by brute appetite. Look around you and you will see that love, for example, has been reduced by millions of young people to the level of the animal. Recent studies in the United States of America have shown that schoolboys commonly use the word 'bitch' as a synonym for girls and that schoolgirls use 'dog' for boys. Courtship is dead and in its place is the desire for instant gratification. A popular T-shirt among teenagers says, 'No More Mr. Nice Guy'. The modern culture around us is the culture of immediate gratification. Rapists are getting younger - under 18's commit one in five of all rapes and under 15's commit one in twenty. Sexual attacks by thirteen and fourteen year olds have doubled in the last decade.

Let me quote Kate Muir, a columnist on 'The Times' of London. She says of this present generation of young people that 'Those lacking parents or at least parents who provide a structure with taboos and traditions laid out before them, are now floating in a soup of uncertainty, relying on animal instinct above common sense.' Note that little phrase, 'Relying on animal instinct above common sense.'

It is pure 'Nebuchadnezzar' isn't it? He forgot God and he started to live by animal instinct. So have millions in our culture.

All around us God's Name is taken in vain, that is, used in conversation so as not to mean anything by it. The Scriptures and the values they teach are ignored by millions. The result is a catastrophic break-down of morality and millions of young people are living by animal instinct above God's value system as set out even in the Ten Commandments of the Old Testament. Human life, even amongst young people, has become cheap. Our culture is the culture of the scruffy, the rude, the obscene. In the United Kingdom the 'Spitting Image' TV programme which mocks and jeers at just about everything is extremely popular. Nothing is sacred any more. If it is it will soon be soaked in a spitting image, nationwide.

The Scriptures show that God was very good to Nebuchadnezzar and restored him to sanity. He came to worship the true God and began to live a dignified and noble life. His sinking into animalistic behaviour, though, is an extremely contemporary message. It warns us to worship only God. As Rabbi Hugo Gryn, President of the Reform Synagogues of Great Britain, said recently of his experiences as a child in the Nazi concentration camp at Auchwitz, where the Nazis forgot God and behaved worse than animals. 'All sorts of things happened to my faith during the Holocaust and although I could not have articulated it in this way, there is one thing that I understood very precisely: what happened to us was not because of what God did but what people did after rejecting Him. I witnessed the destruction that follows when men try to turn themselves into gods.' ('A Childhood,' Rabbi Hugo Gryn, The Times Magazine, Sat. July 31, 1993).

So it is that the story of Nebuchadnezzar teaches us that none of us is big enough to be the goal of our own existence. Nebuchadnezzar had boasted as though the source of all the lovely things around him were in himself. He didn't credit God with giving him the gifts that he had. Surely gifts are meant to lead us back to God in gratitude. Whether those gifts be a lovely farm, a university degree, a fine business, a healthy family, a gifted church, or whatever, we must give God the glory for those things that are given to us.

Nebuchadnezzar's story also tells us that we cannot live in God's world and reject God and suppose that mankind is going to retain its dignity, beauty and glory. His story also, thankfully, shows us that when God is given His place in any individual's or nation's life, health, sanity and true beauty return.

CHAPTER FIVE

VALUES
in politics & pleasure

Nothing dominates world headlines in our generation like politics. The rise and fall of governments are meat and drink to the media and every nuance of political life is catalogued. Polls as to government's popularity or otherwise, are taken regularly, long before governments are tested at the ballot box. Conversation everywhere is peppered with views on presidents, prime ministers or members of governments from Bangkok to Washington, from Paris to Tokyo.

God, also, has revealed his view of government and this is highlighted in Daniel chapter 2 and also in chapter 7. In chapter 2 governments are depicted as a beautiful work of art, in the image of man. In chapter 7 there is a very vivid contrast. The very same governments are depicted as ferocious, wild beasts. Are the two view contradictory? Certainly not. You need to get a picture of both if you want to understand what God thinks of government. In Daniel chapter 2, the feet of the image of man is made of iron and clay which simply will not mix. The whole structure proves to be impossible to unite, permanently. In Daniel chapter 7 the governments of the world are likened to beasts and they are put away, not because they are weak but because they are strong and possessed of such frightening power that had God let them go on, they would have destroyed mankind completely and the planet on which we live.

In our generation it is vital that we learn from God's assessment of Gentile government. It is not that God thinks all governments and their politics are useless and downright bad. Who would want to go back to caveman days? Governments like the Roman government built superb roads, the Greeks brought incredible inventions, Napoleon's code is still the basic legal code of France. Other governments have made incredible strides in the whole field of social justice, medicine and health care, aviation development, etc. Yet, in chapter 2 of Daniel God is saying that though governments are often very good, they are all, despite their good qualities, impermanent. The fact is that no matter how great the empire or government, they all come and go. The British Empire, for example, was supposed to last a thousand years but it proved to be one of the shortest in history. God is saying that no political structure is of absolute value. We must not exalt things that are of relative value and treat them as if they were of absolute value. Even democracy with all of its virtues is by no means perfect. Governments are, as the image of Daniel 2, unstable. Why? Because although they are good at making promises, they are not good a keeping them all. They try but there is not one that hasn't failed in this area, whether led by presidents, kings, queens or prime ministers and their cabinets.

Governments, of course, can be extremely wicked. Like ferocious animals, governments under Napoleon, Stalin, Hitler, Pol Pot, Saddam Hussein or whoever, have sought to subjugate people across history. From Argentina to Vietnam, from the Balkans to the ethnic wars of the former Soviet Union, we can see very clearly hat government can be indescribably ruthless. Daniel chapter 7 shows very clearly that the Messiah will come one day and remove government and set up His own kingdom. Let us stand up, then, in our generation for the great value of the truth of the return of Christ. Our planet is not going to be left to wreck and ruin or at the ultimate mercy of some maniac of a world leader with his finger on genetic engineering or nuclear warheads. There is coming to this earth the great kingdom of our Lord and Saviour, Jesus Christ. When it comes it will be stable and permanent and will fulfil, to the letter, all the promises made of it. "I was", wrote Daniel, "Watching in the night visions, and behold, one like the Son of Man coming with the clouds of heaven! He came to the Ancient of Days and they brought Him near before Him. Then to Him was given dominion and glory and a kingdom, that all peoples, nations, languages should serve Him. His dominion is an everlasting dominion, which shall not pass away, and His kingdom the one which shall not be destroyed". (Daniel 7: 13-14).

What Daniel saw was no fantasy. It was no fairy story to comfort him in the dark with unrealistic hope. Neither is the value of the truth unreliable, today. Here is our hope! The Lord Jesus is coming again! The message is that we must not debate or dispute its truth. We must believe it and live it and stand fast.

Belshazzar, Nebuchadnezzar's dynastic son, didn't believe a word of it. One night with a thousand of his lords, he displayed what he thought about life's supreme value. He showed to the world around him that he reckoned life's supreme value was having a good time. He knew of God's value system, the evidence had been clear in Nebuchadnezzar's life, but he chose to ignore it. In the midst of a magnificent feast, he made a decision. God and His value system had annoyed him, so, in the midst of his feast he had the sacred Hebrew vessels which Nebuchadnezzar had taken from the temple which had been in Jerusalem brought to the feast and he and his lords, his wives, and his concubines drank from them. It was a blasphemy and he knew it, but so what? Like our generation where the top swear words are "God" and "Christ", he thumbed his nose at God and got on with his riotous party. Who cared? In his view the whole thing was nonsense anyway. Life was a cabaret, old chum, come to the cabaret.

God and His value system aren't nonsense, though, are they? Right in the middle of his party the Eternal broke into time and the fingers of a man's hand wrote upon the plaster of the wall of his banqueting chamber. Belshazzar's countenance changed, his hips were loosened and his knees knocked against each other. Why Because he couldn't understand the writing. Yes, it was simple enough; it said, "A minor, a minor, a shekel and half a shekel". He had seen those words often, before In those days they did not have coins for money but weighed out gold and silve on a pair of scales. The phrase was a phrase of weights.

Why, then, was Belshazzar afraid? If a finger of a man's had wrote pounds and pence or dollars and cents or pesetas or ruples on your wall and you had reason to believe it was God's hand that wrote it, would you not be worried? Eventually Daniel was called and the message from God was hauntingly plain. Belshazzar had counted God valueless, now it was God's turn to evaluate him and he was weighed in God's balance and found, wanting. That night a raiding army invaded Babylon and Belshazzar died and his culture, entourage and power were overthrown. The wine was drunk, the crumbs from his table covered the floor, the plates were dirty; the party was all over. Life proved to be no cabaret after all. God and His value system proved to be much more permanent.

It was many years later that God's value system was perfectly described by the Lord Jesus. He told the story of the three lost things; a shepherd who lost a sheep, the lady who lost the coin, the man who lost his son. Now sheep are valuable, and so the shepherd left his ninety-nine safe sheep to find his lost one. Money though is more valuable than sheep and the lady who lost her coin never stopped until she shad swept out her house and found it. If sheep are valuable and money is more valuable, what about an individual? If, on a ship, a cry goes up, "Man overboard", nobody enquires whether it is a good man or a bad man, a young man or an old man, a rich man or a poor man. They don't say, "Is he a Labour Party supporter or a Conservative Party supporter?" "Is he a Democrat or a Republican?" "Is he a Catholic or a Protestant, a Hindu or a Moslem?" "Was he in first class or second class?" "Was he a member of the crew?" Nobody worries, in that moment, about such things. The point is that an individual is lost and to save that individual, all available equipment is employed and every conceivable effort exhausted. The loss of a person is the dizziest pinnacle of tragedy. Truth is, the whole world wouldn't pay for the value of a soul and it was the Lord Jesus who said, "What shall it profit a man if he should gain the whole world and lose his own soul?" The answer is, nothing.

The Lord Jesus shed His precious blood at Calvary in order to pay the debt of ur sin and if we repent towards God and put faith in the Lord Jesus we can know rue salvation and start living for the values that really last. Never were those values nore needed than they are in our society today.

'Am I a soldier of the cross,
A follower of the Lamb?
And shall I fear to own His cause,
Or blush to speak His Name?'

CHAPTER SIX

VALUES
have consequences

A very sinister element now enters the story of Daniel. As Daniel lives out his life for God, applying God's value system in his every day work as a high official in Babylon, some very nasty individuals set to work to undermine him. Their value system was the law of the jungle where Daniel, they reckoned, was treading on their territory and they wanted rid of him.

"But," says the Scripture, "They could find no charge or fault because he was faithful: nor was there any error of fault found in him". These wicked leaders then decided the only way they could bring any charge against Daniel was to find against him in the area of his faith. They persuaded the new ruler of Babylon, King Darius, to establish a decree that "Whoever petitions any god or man for thirty-one days, except you, O King, shall be cast into a den of lions". The very sinister sting in the tail came when they declared, "Now O King, establish the decree and sign the writing, so that it cannot be changed, according to the law of the Medes and Persians which does not alter".

We have come a long way in our study from Nebuchadnezzar who, despite his many faults, had respect for other people's faith. Now see a sinister introduction of a written law which bans the worship of anything other than the state and what it dictates. In the English language the little phrase "It's the law of the Medes and Persians" means, to this very day, "It can't be changed".

Later in the book of Daniel we see a power rise which removes Israel's right to daily worship in their temple (See Daniel 8: 9-12) and this has portents of the coming fearful ruler which the world will yet see, the Anti-Christ (see 2 Thessalonians 3-12). Daniel's experience of facing the written law banning him from worshipping the Lord is but a cameo of what is coming upon the world. We see syncretism all around us at the moment. Syncretism teaches that all religions have some essential insight that we all need, whatever we have been brought up in. Syncretism denies that Christ is the exclusive way to God and frowns upon any who claim that he is. Syncretists detest Christ's claim when He said, "I am the way, the truth and the life, no-one comes unto the Father but by Me". (John 14: 6). Soon syncretists will not just frown on people who teach the exclusiveness of Christ as the only Saviour, they will push to legislate against them.

Soon they will not just treat as anti-social Christians who hold to the values of the Saviour as the only Mediator between God and men. (See 1 Timothy 2: 5). They will see to it that they are treated as law breakers. The Scripture shows that the Anti-Christ, the coming world ruler, will link up the world's religions and the world's politics into one great monolithic structure and any not bowing to the Anti-Christ will be crushed. A huge drive towards political and economic union of states that we see today will eventually involve a religious union as well. Dire will be the consequence for any standing in its way.

Our present freedom to worship in the West is a very precious freedom and we should be grateful to any government that encapsulates that freedom in law. But cripture shows that such freedom will not always be available.

In his most helpful and inspiring little book, "Time To Wake Up!", (Evangelical ess, Pages 140-141), Leith Samuel lists five aspects which make the Christian ith absolutely unique and Bible believers, who look to the Scripture as their final thority in all matters of belief and practice, desperately need to understand again e value of these aspects of their faith and stand up for them with love, compassion, ut determined courage in days when syncretism would seek to swamp them. For any believers who hold to these beliefs and teach them, death is a very real ossibility in many parts of the world, even now.

This is particularly true where militant Islam holds sway. Written, constitu-onal law, like the law of Darius the Mede in Daniel's day, demands it. What are ose aspects that are so costly to hold and yet so precious? They are;

"Firstly, the Christian faith is the only faith in the world which offers the dividual a direct personal relationship with the Holy, sinless founder of the faith.

Secondly, the Christian faith is the only faith in the world which offers the rgiveness of sins at the expense of the Founder of the faith.

Thirdly, the Christian faith is the only faith in the world which offers eternal life s a free gift now, through the grace of the Founder of the faith.

Fourthly, the Christian faith is the only faith in the world which allows you to ring nothing, nothing but you sins, salvation is entirely undeserved. We have ome to God on God's terms, or not at all.

Fifthly, the Christian faith alone clearly shows the futility of standing on tip-toe ying to reach up to God. The Gospel tells us that it was God in His loving kindness nd sheer mercy who reached down to us in our guilt and need. (See Ephesians 2: -10 and Titus 3: 3-7)."

Daniel, of course, written law or not, refused to stop worshipping the Lord. Note he detail of Scripture. "Now when Daniel knew that the writing was signed, he vent home. And in his upper room, with his windows open towards Jerusalem, he nelt down on his knees three times that day, and prayed and gave thanks before is God, as was his custom since early days". Daniel was discovered by his enemies nd reported to the King. The King, when he heard about Daniel, "Laboured until he going down of the sun to deliver him" but the written law he had signed couldn't e changed. There was, it seemed, no deliverance. He had signed a law refusing nan the right to worship his Creator. Daniel was thrown into the den of lions. As

my friend Rowland Pickering once pointed out, "There is a huge differen
between a den of lions and a lion's den; one could be empty but the other couldn'
He is right. Daniel went into the den of lions and that seemed to be the end of th

But no. The God who made man intervenes in history. He shuts the lion
mouths and reverses the law of the jungle and Daniel is delivered to see t
conversion of King Darius himself. (See Daniel 6: 25-27)! It is absolutely thrillin
to read the Scriptures and discover that in Christ's coming world kingdom, He, th
Messiah, will do the same again.

The Messiah will, in fact, intervene in history once more and defeat the An
Christ and all his laws and "Then the kingdom and dominion, and the greatness
the kingdoms under the whole heaven, shall be given to the people, the saints
the Most High. His kingdom is an everlasting kingdom, and all its dominions sha
serve and obey Him." (See Daniel 7: 23-27). In that coming kingdom the law
the jungle will be reversed for we read that then, "The wolf also shall dwell wi
the lamb, the leopard shall lie down with the young goat, the calf and the young lic
and the fatling together; and a little child shall lead them. The cow and the bear sha
graze; their young ones shall lie down together; and the lion shall eat straw like th
ox. The nursing child shall play by the cobra's hole and the weaned child shall p
his hand into the viper's den. They shall not hurt or destroy in all my holy mountai
for the earth shall be full of the knowledge of the Lord as the waters cover the se
And in that day there shall be a Root of Jesse, who shall stand as a banner to th
people; for the Gentiles shall seek Him, and His resting place shall be glorious"
(Isaiah 11: 6-10). Today we pray that God's Will be done on earth as it is in heaver
then our prayers will be answered.

Values, of course, have consequences. The wicked men in Darius' kingdor
who had lived according to the value of the law of the jungle, now died by it. W
read that the King gave command and brought those men who had accused Danie
and cast them into the den of lions and "The lions overpowered them and broke al
their bones in pieces before then ever came to the bottom of the den". The law o
the jungle was not changed for those who were determined to live by it. Nor wil
it ever be.

I remember very well being taken by some Christians to visit the streets o
Hollywood, California. Millions of people, I was told, go to Hollywood to try t
capture something of what they think is the true magic of fame, fortune an

reatness. A more boring place you could not find. In fact the Mayor of Hollywood ecided that he would have to create something on the streets of Hollywood to try) make them interesting for the visitors who were pouring into the city. He decided) place metal stars on the pavements encapsulating the names of those people in ie United States of America who were deemed to have "made it". I walked on iose pavements and studied the names and eventually came to the famous Chinese heatre outside which many famous film stars had place an imprint of their hand r feet or foot or arm in wet cement. For fun I placed my foot in the footprints of he famous stars and as I do so, I began to wonder what a true star really was.

The place had no magic for me because my mind suddenly went to the end of he book of Daniel where we read that God spoke to His servant to whom He had aught His value system. God gave Daniel a great vision of future world events and hen told him to go back to his work as an outstanding civil servant and promised im a great inheritance after death. Notice that Daniel, believing in the coming Messiah, did not withdraw from life and activity waiting around for the Lord's eturn. He got on with his work and his belief in God and his value system helped im to be of enormous benefit to the people in the community around him. Yet, God eminded him of what a true star really is. God's beautiful encouraging words to)aniel burned in my mind that night as I stood in Hollywood; "Those who are wise ihall shine like the brightness of the firmament, and those who turn many to ightcousness like the stars for ever and ever". Wouldn't you like to be that kind)f star? I would.

I trust this study of God's value system has helped you to see the fact that God's /alues are truly permanent and worth living for. I leave with you a personal incident which has long etched itself into my mind. I was driving through Portadown in Northern Ireland one day when I suddenly felt an urge to see a friend who was ill. 'God and see Norman", said a voice within me. "But you may be in the way", said another voice. "I was sick and you visited me", said a scripture tucked away somewhere in the back of my mind. I turned my car on the road and drove to his home. Norman greeted me weeping. "I was just asking God to send you to me", he said. While Norman's good wife got the kettle boiling we overhauled the universe together. "Have you ever thought of the verse, '… and it came to pass?'", asked Norman. "It certainly occurs hundreds of times in the Bible", I answered. "Yes, but have you thought about it?", he asked, insistently. "Fame comes … to pass. Money comes ... to pass. Suffering comes ... to pass. Rain comes ... to pass. Sunshine comes ... to pass". He listed many things in life which come to pass. Then he paused for breath.

"What about the things that come to stay?", my friend then asked. Around the crackling Ulster fireside we quietly gathered our little bunch of everlasting. Forgiveness of sins comes to stay. Salvation comes to stay. Jesus Christ Himself is the same yesterday, today and for ever. When He enters a life, He certainly comes to stay.

A few weeks later I preached Norman's text at his graveside. While I spoke on the theme "... and it came to pass" Norman was enjoying the indescribable presence of the One whose love will never end and whose value system is indescribably worth following. May God give us grace in these crisis days in our world to live for the things which are eternal. May our lifestyles and our behaviour mirror, in a desperately needy world, God's value system. As Daniel proved it to be trustworthy, so can we.